CREATIVE IDEAS FOR KIDS PRAYER

Colleen Clabaugh

DEDICATION

To those willing to invest in children and youth.

CONTENTS

INTRODUCTION

I think a lot about prayer. When I was a kid my mother prayed, so as a child, I too I learned to pray. As I grew older I tried to "perfect" prayer and I learned to teach others how to pray. Then one day I actually listened to that deep, nagging voice in the crevices of my soul that was whispering, *"You don't really know what you are doing, do you? There's more to this... more to prayer."* It was then that I took a step back from everything I knew, everything I learned, everything I taught, and all the voices around me still trying to tell me how to do it "right" and I became ... a child.

As we get older most of us feel as if we've attained some wealth of knowledge, whether through books, mentors, teachers or experience. We gather all of those nuggets and give ourselves labels to qualify our positions such as parent, grandparent, teacher, mentor, leader, etc. We ground ourselves in our own knowledge and find security in our wisdom. Still yet, we hear that little voice whispering, *"There's more to this!"*

It took a great adversity in my life to bring me to the reality that most things I thought I knew about prayer were simply incomplete - not incorrect, but incomplete. I knew the methods. I knew the "Our Father" prayer pattern. I knew the reasons why prayers may or may not get answered. I knew how to pray, why to pray, and when to pray. Still, it was incomplete. Still I longed for something more. Still I heard the whisper.

Jesus said, *"Except ye be converted, and become as little children, ye shall not enter into the kingdom of heaven"* (Matthew 18:3). Children have an innate ability to see life through simplicity and imagination that spark creativity and wild adventures. They believe easily. They imagine boundlessly. They converse with excitement and listen to stories with eyes wide. They become open doors to worlds of possibility. In times of prayer they don't get caught up in 9-step programs, loud repetitions, or lofty words.

Since working with the Kids Prayer ministry, I've purposefully began to listen to the prayers of children. I've heard children pray a ten word sentence that was powerful. They have a way of being simple, yet direct. They pray just as well with their eyes wide open as with them tightly shut. They sometimes fidget, while at the same time hear God speak to them. In simplest terms, they just talk to God with faith, pray His Word, and accept that He will answer whatever way He chooses.

Somehow the simplicity of that removed all the stress I had experienced earlier in my life that left me feeling I wasn't doing it hard enough, right enough, or often enough. I found myself free - free to pray and just talk to God without all the rules that my "adultness" had tacked on. Can it really be that simple? I learned, "Yes; a conversation with God is that simple!"

The next time you grab a phone to call a friend, or you sit down to write an email to a family member, or you text your BFF a message on your phone, ask yourself, *"What about my conversation or message was so hard for me to physically do?"* Your answer will most likely be, *"Nothing."*

Don't you think God deserves the same? Prayer doesn't have to be difficult. Watch a child; you'll be amazed at what they can teach you. But be prepared for an adventure because when God says that He can do *"exceeding abundantly above all that we ask or think,"* they will simply believe Him, and He alone with get the credit. It's that simple.

- Colleen Clabaugh

On the following pages are simple ways that you can train your children or kids prayer group to pray. They are simple, they are effective, and they work.

TICK-TOCK PRAYER CLOCK

Even if you have a heart for prayer, you may sometimes run out of ideas that help you talk with Jesus. Use this prayer clock to help train your brain to pray!

The clock covers time slots for:
- Petition
- Adoration
- Intercession
- Confession

You may download the prayer clock at:
http://www.kidsprayer.com/adults/ideas/tick-tock-prayer-clock/

SWEET-N-SOUR GRAB BAGS

Prepare one grab bag with several different kinds of candy—sweet, sour, hot, and dark chocolate—one bag for every four kids. Form groups of four and give each group a grab bag. Have children take turns reaching into the bag for one piece of candy. When each child has a treat, explain that the candies represent different kinds of prayer. Use the following examples to lead kids in prayer.

Sweet candy—Thank God for his many blessings

Sour candy—Ask God to bless those who are bitter from hurts in their life. Repent over any sins you've done. Forgive and pray for those who have done you wrong.

Hot candy—Ask God to keep you excited about serving him. Pray for revival.

Dark-chocolate candy—Pray for someone who's going through a difficult time. Pray for direction.

After you've prayed, enjoy the treats.

GLOBAL PRAYERS

Have a group of kids sit in a circle. Toss an inflatable globe to one of the children. Instruct them that wherever their forefinger lands, they are to pray for that country. If their finger lands on water, then pray for people in various islands. The main purpose of this is to teach the children to pray Kingdom prayers—those that are not for themselves or their own family and friends.

You can also use a large ball that is made in the design of a globe as an alternative. Add in music for added fun – when the music stops, whoever has the globe has to pray.

You may purchase cheap inflatable globes online or at places such as Oriental Trading.

PIN-THE-PRAYER

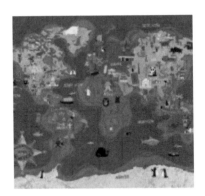

Earlier, we mentioned the idea of using an inflatable globe as a creative prayer tool for kids. Sometimes kids can get more focused on throwing the globe around than praying, so if this is your situation, try this alternative method.

Get a large map that has continents and country names on it. Blindfold the child, then play Pin-the-Prayer-on-the-Prayer-Map (similar to Pin-the-Tail-on-the-Donkey). Wherever the pin lands (or their finger) talk about that country, what their lifestyles are like, their religious beliefs, and then pray for the people of that area.

"OPERATION" PRAYER

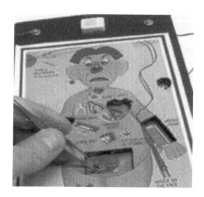

One of the fun things that kids like to play is the old "Operation" game. The game board has a human body on it with little areas cut out where strategic body parts such as the heart and stomach go. The goal is to get all the body pieces out of the hole (like a surgeon) without touching the metal edge of the opening. If you do touch the metal opening you will be buzzed and lose your turn.

There are hundreds of people all over our cities with physical ailments, and those who need surgery. You can use this game to have the child select a person with an ailment similar to the body piece of the game they are trying to remove. Pray over that need and if they get buzzed, keep praying for that person until someone gets the part out without being buzzed.

You can also pray simple prayers of blessing over these parts of the body, including such things as God touching our minds (brain) with wisdom in our decisions and situations we face.

I SPY GOD

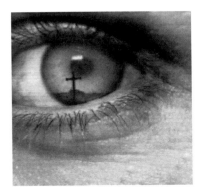

How do you pray to someone that you cannot see? How can you believe in something you can't touch? Does God really even exist at all? If you've ask these questions, the answer is all around you, it just takes a little effort to see it.

Have the children sit in a group in a large room where there are various things to look at. Start the activity by saying something such as, "I spy God... in the lights above our head." The children may get quizzical looks when you say that until you explain that God is our "light and our salvation," or, "God gives us understanding and helps us to see what is right and wrong." Go around the room allowing the children to "spy God" in the things they see. You can also take your group outdoors for even more ways to view God.

A young boy in one kids prayer group said he spied God in the door of the classroom—"God is the door to salvation." Another girl said she spied God in the books on the table—"God gives us knowledge and wisdom."

As the children begin to spy God around them their praise and worship experience with God will grow because they will see Him in big ways and in things that are around them every day. Have the kids write down a new way that they spied God that week and share with the group the next time you meet.

This is a great game for families to use while driving, including moms and dads. Not only is it fun, but it creates opportunities for families to talk about God the way Deuteronomy chapter six told us to.

HOPSCOTCH AND A PRAYER

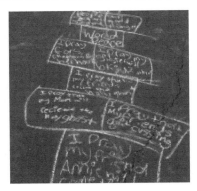

A fun idea for outdoor praying is using a sidewalk or driveway and drawing a hopscotch board with caulk. In each block, let the child write in a prayer request.

For Kingdom praying, use a different country for each box, or a different people group, such as Muslims, Hindus, Buddhists, Tribal groups, orphans, or the unreached peoples.

When the child is ready to play, they throw a rock into the hopscotch area and hop to the box the rock landed in and pray for that request. If you have a group of children, you can let them each write a prayer in a different box so children are praying for other children's requests.

Keep playing until all boxes have been prayed over. If a box has been become too blurred to read, then erase it and write a new request.

It's a great way to pray while they play!

KEEP THEM PRAYING ALL WEEK

One of the hardest things to do in Kids Prayer is to keep your kids praying throughout the week when they are not all together in your prayer group or at church. Some families do not practice prayer at home, or may feel awkward doing it with their children if they don't know what to do or how to pray very well themselves.

One way to handle this is to notify and get permission from the parents for the kids to have their own phone tree. At a designated time during the early evening, start the phone tree by calling the first child and telling them what the topic for prayer is that day and any additional prayer requests. Depending on the age, that child can call and tell the next child, or you or your staff can call each one. It should only take a few moments per child, and this will help to get the parents support and involvement as well.

You can also take prayer requests from the child or family. Most people are appreciative when someone takes the time to ask if they need prayer. They may not always have a request to give you but be sure one day they will have an important one, and they will be waiting for your call.

WE ARE ALL ONE BODY

We are all one part of the body of Christ—the Church. There are teachers, preachers, evangelists, musicians, and more who work together to fulfill the plan of God. Just as our body cannot function correctly with just a hand or a foot, one person alone cannot do all the work of God (1 Corinthians 12). We each have a purpose and role that God wants us to fulfill with our life.

Take an ordinary Mr. or Ms. Potato Head toy. Place all the pieces in a bag or something the kids can reach into. Have them one by one pull out a different piece. Have them come up with a prayer to pray using the item they choose.

For example, if they picked the shoes, they can pray that God would lead us to people that we can tell about the Lord, or pray that God would guide our decisions and the paths we take in life. Have them place their piece into the potato where it's not supposed to go.

After all the pieces have been put in the potato will look silly. Use this to remind the children that we need to do what God asks us to do, not necessarily what we want to do. If we don't our lives may end up looking like the silly potato head where things just don't work right.

PICTURE ALBUM PRAYERS

For small children, make a picture album for them to use during prayer time. Pictures are easier to use since they may not be able to read or write well yet. Put in various photos of family, a homeless person (symbolizing the poor), different people groups of the world, etc. Include pictures of every day blessings to give thanks for: food, clothing, a home, etc. Their requests can also be put into picture form: grandmother, father, swing set, new bike, and so on.

Each day, have them pray over different sets of pictures and be sure to change out the pictures from time to time to keep their interest.

You may wish to create picture albums for the older kids, or different themes to use throughout the year. Each week, insert a picture representing something that your group is praying for that week. For example, if a major disaster has struck and your child or group is praying about it that week, print out pictures of the topic and put into your album. You can use a scrapbook album to give an area for the child to write their prayer request in beside the photo. Every so often, review the album with the child(ren) or your church and give thanks to God for whatever He has done regarding the requests.

NEWSPAPER PRAYERS

Have kids bring in copies of recent city or national newspapers. Go through the pages and find articles that reference things and issues that kids can pray over. Don't limit the kids to just those on violence or crime but consider praying for political issues, community awareness, education, etc. When you see an article on something good pray that God can be glorified in some way in it and that those things would continue according to His will.

You can also pray over the supermarket ads for God to provide food to the homeless in your area or for God to work in our current economic situation so families can afford their basic necessities without resorting to crime. When you come across advertisements for ungodly things such as alcohol, drugs, etc, pray that God and the city would shut down those venues or sources. (Be careful on what you discuss with children.)

You can create a book to put cut-out articles in or pin them to a wall for the kids to lay their hands on and pray over.

HUNTING FOR TREASURE

During the Easter season egg hunts abound. Children are used to getting candy, money, toys or other such things as prizes from the eggs they collect, but why not give them the treasure of God's Word? An easy way to incorporate prayer into the holiday activities is to put scriptures or prayer requests on pieces of paper in plastic eggs and then hide them around the room, church, or outdoors. When children find the eggs they can pray the scripture inside over someone they know or over some need that they are aware of. You can put the name of a person or a need on the back of the scripture so they can easily know whom, or for what, to pray the verse over. As an added treat, include a piece of candy in the egg so they will want to find as many as possible.

If time permits, you can gather the eggs back together and play Hot-Eggs *(like the game Hot-Potato).* You can also play music while passing the egg around, and stop the music so whoever has the egg can pray. There a ton of ways to use the eggs, just make sure to include the scriptures and requests in the mix (and candy)!

NATIONAL DAY OF PRAYER

It is God's will for Christians to be good citizens. We are to obey the laws of the land, we are to respect those in public office, and we are to pray for government officials. The annual National Day of Prayer is a great opportunity for kids to get involved in something that is bigger than just their local church group or family. As you train your kids to pray, have them pray over their nation's leaders; this is pleasing to God. Here are some things you can have them pray over:

PRESIDENT AND ADVISORS

Lord, help our president and his advisors to have courage to make good decisions for our nation, even if it's not popular. Put people around him that have good morals and want to do what's right in your eyes. Remind them at they are to be good examples to us. Talk to them and draw them to you so that they can find salvation and be filled with your Spirit. Protect him and keep him safe.

GOVERNORS AND CITY LEADERS

Lord, help our city and state leaders that they will do what's best for us, and not what's best for themselves. Help to know how to promote peace in our communities. Give our judges and leaders wisdom to make laws and would benefit the city and the people but not hurt our churches. Help to keep Christian advisors around them and be the best leaders they can be for us.

MILITARY TROOPS & COMMUNITY SAFETY WORKERS

Lord, please watch over our troops as they protect us and our people. Give their families peace and comfort while they are gone. Help our police officers, firemen, hospital workers and other workers to make our communities safe and peaceful to live in. Protect them, and bring them home to their families safely. Draw them to you so they can feel your love and find salvation.

PRAYING FOR THE SICK...KID-STYLE

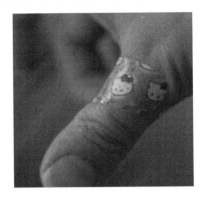

Often in our kids prayer group we receive requests to pray for people that need healing. Most of these requests are for people that our kids don't often come in contact with, so in the past we have sent these sick people a prayer cloth, just like the apostles did in the New Testament. We like for people to know that the prayer cloth came from the kids group so we have used brightly colored or patterned material. Lately we have been using different things for prayer cloths.

When a kid skins their knee they automatically feel better once they have a Band-Aid on. For these purposes our group uses kid friendly (fun) Band-Aids as prayer cloths. We anoint the gauze on the Band-Aid and pray over it just as we would a piece of cloth.

Another thing that we have used is get well cards. We either purchase one or have the kids make one. After taking time to write a message and sign the card, the kids pray for the person receiving it.

Another prayer cloth we have used is probably the most fun. There was a prayer request for someone who had recently been diagnosed with cancer. We printed off a coloring page for the part of the body where the cancer is and then used poster paint on our hands and laid hands on the paper where the cancer was and prayed for healing.

WAILIING WALL

The Wailing Wall (often referenced also as the area of the Gate of Mercy) is a remnant of an ancient wall that surrounded the Jewish Temple's courtyard in Old Jerusalem, and is one of the most sacred places in Judaism. It has been a site for Jewish prayers and pilgrimages for centuries. Many of those who come to pray at the walls write prayers on slips of paper and press them into the cracks. More than one millions prayers are pressed into these cracks each year.

A great way to use this in kids prayer is to create a "wailing wall" and have the kids write their own prayer requests. The wall can be as simple as a piece of corkboard that prayer requests are tacked to, or you can make a wall out of foam with "cracks" melted into it. If you have time and space, you can create a whole wall in a classroom or prayer area for this purpose.

Some children may feel apprehensive about leaving prayer requests on the wall that are sensitive in nature. You can explain to them that any such prayer requests should be written on the inside of a slip of paper, and then folded over so no one can see the inside. On the outside of the request, have the children write what type of prayer request it is, whether it's for healing, salvation, or other. As the children put their request on the wall, go over scriptures that they can pray over their request to get them used to praying biblical prayers.

POPCORN PRAYERS

The closer children feel they are to God, the stronger their relationship can be with Him.

Divide the children equally and have them stand in two lines, facing each other, about 10 feet apart. Each child will need to be facing another child. The children will be tossing a piece of popcorn back and forth to the person across from them. If you have an odd number of children, the extra child can count the number of successful catches.

Give all the children in the first row, called row "A", a piece of popcorn, and tell them that on your signal, they will toss the piece of popcorn 10 feet across to the person directly facing them in row "B". Instruct the older children to use only one hand to toss or catch the popcorn. Tell the kids that the popcorn in this activity represents our relationship with God. Give the signal and have the children toss the popcorn. Many of the tosses will fall short since the children are so far apart. Record the number of successful throws on a chalkboard or whiteboard.

Make sure each child in row "B" has a piece of popcorn. Each child in row "B" will take one-step towards row "A". Then on your signal, have the children toss the popcorn again. Once again, record the number of successful throws on a chalkboard or whiteboard. Do this several more times, each time taking one-step closer until the two rows are together. Once together, the children can simply drop the popcorn into the hands of the other child, resulting in no misses.

Explain that our relationship with God is similar to what we just did. The further away from each other, the harder it was to catch the popcorn. Likewise, the further we are from God, the harder it is to have a relationship with Him. On the other hand, the closer we are to God, the easier it will be to have a strong relationship with Him.

How do we get close to God? We can get closer to God by reading the Bible, praying, and fasting.

VIRTUAL PRAYER WALKS

Prayer walking helps you become aware of situations in an area that you may not be aware of. Many times we drive through parts of our towns without taking notice of what is happening. We may not even be aware of all the types of businesses along our daily routes. The same can be true of our prayers for other countries. Something that can create awareness of needs in another country is a virtual prayer walk. These walks are actually very easy to put together and you would not need to leave your home town to prayer walk in China, Africa, South America, Europe, Australia, Central America or even the town 30 miles away.

One way you can have a virtual prayer walk is to make posters using clip art representing architecture in the place you are focusing on. If you have access to an overhead projector you can trace the image onto poster board and color. Another way is to collect photos from the area and print them off on 8.5 x 11 paper. You can insert pictures into a Power Point presentation for classroom display and focused prayer.

JELLY BEAN CANDY PRAYERS

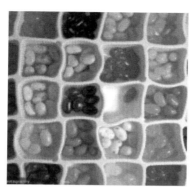

Easter means the aisles of your local store is full of brightly or pastel colored candy. Many kids get baskets on Easter full of this same candy. Instead of just letting the kids get cavities or fight over who ate the bunny's ears let's teach them how to pray with some of it. A favorite at this time of year is Jelly Beans.

SPECKLED: represents how sin separate us from God.

RED: is for the blood God shed, a sacrifice only He could pay.

WHITE: represents the cleansing of our soul as God washes our sins away.

BLUE: is for water baptism, an outward expression of our faith and obedience.

YELLOW: represents hope and heaven that we are waiting for!

GREEN: is for the spiritual growth we achieve, as we study God's Word and get close to Him.

PRAYER POCKET PILLOW CASES

Have your kids make a prayer pocket on a pillowcase. They can sew the pocket on, use fabric glue or some other type of strong adhesive, or have an adult assist them in tacking it on some other way. Each night, they should write out a prayer and put it in their prayer pocket while they "sleep on it."

The message is that while we may be sleeping, God never sleeps, and always watches over us, bringing us peace and comfort when we trust in Him. And since it's a pillow, prayer is the last thing we do at night and the first thing we do when we get up in the morning!

THANKSGIVING POST-IT NOTES

During a chosen day, carry around a pen and post-it notes. Make an effort to jot down every time something positive happens or you are aware of a reason to thank God. This might include:

• for the sun, which provides the energy to run the planet

• for having a house to wake up in, and food for breakfast

• for having transportation to get to school / work

• for some kind words spoken to you during the day

If you really thought about it, you would probably run out of post-it notes! By the end of the day you may have a whole pad of blessings.

Often we make a habit of only noticing bad things that happen, and gradually forget about the good things that surround us daily. This exercise can help alter our perspective from the 'glass half empty' to the 'glass half full' mentality. Understandably, there might be days or long periods of time when you may feel that there is little to be thankful for at all. Perhaps you have been unwell or unemployed for a long time? Perhaps you have difficulties with your family or job? If so, you might find yourself thinking, 'Well, that's o.k. for you, but what about my situation?' You may find this exercise emotionally difficult, but on the other hand, it might help you to recognize some of the good things you do have, and feel a bit more positive. Often it is the people who face the most trying of circumstances who are examples to others for their ability to realize how much there is to be thankful for, even in hard times.

As you form the habit of looking for God's blessings, your children will often follow. Be sure to be vocal about sharing the blessings you've received and have them do the same. You can even make a game out of it, to see who can find or share the most blessings in a day.

LETTERS TO GOD

Some people find it easier to write down their feelings than to verbalize them. Try writing a letter to God, expressing what's going on in your life and mind. You might want to say that you are sorry for something, or there may be a situation you just can't understand and want to pour out your feelings. Maybe you want to make a promise to God to do something in particular, or to change a habit.

Often we can find that writing something down helps us to understand it or deal with it better. By writing specifically to God, you accomplish all of the above and leave it in His hands – the best hands to deal with it!

Keep your letters in a journal for later reflection.

GOOD-NIGHT PRAYER

Have each child chose three friends to pray for whom you would love to come to know Jesus. Give the kids three glow-in-the-dark stars to stick on the ceiling above their beds as prayer reminders. Every night when they switch their light off, those three stars will glow, reminding them to pray. The stars will also remind them of those three special people whom God loves (like all of Abraham's descendants –as many as stars in the sky).

You can also include one special star representing the child, as reminder that they too are God's child and He never stops caring or thinking about them.

SENDING BALLOONS TO HEAVEN

This is a fun group activity, particularly for children, though anyone can enjoy it! You will need an assortment of balloons and a tank of helium. Write names and/or prayers for people who are overseas onto pieces of paper that you stuff into the balloons. You may inflate the balloon and write them on the outside of the balloon instead, if you wish.

At a specific time have everyone release the balloons, praying together. It is a good symbol of the 'prayers of the saints' ascending up to heaven for God to answer.

You could even write your address/email address (with parental permission) onto a balloon and see if you get a response from someone finding it!

GIVING COMPLIMENTS

It's important for children to learn how to complement each other so that they will know how to compliment God during their times of praise and worship.

Depending on the ages of the children in your group this can be hard to do. Boys are afraid to say something nice to girls and vice versa for fear of "cooties"; however it is important that they participate. If they can freely complement each other it will become easier for them to compliment God which is the core of praise and worship.

Have the children sit in a circle with a chair in the center. Then one at a time have each child sit in the center chair. Have the children in the circle take turns giving compliments to the one in the center. This may be compliments on their looks, character, their friendship, their skills or abilities, or just random thoughts.

Repeat this until all the children have had a turn. The more they work on this the easier it will become, and it boosts their self-esteems and ability to believe that God can work through their life.

IN IT, NOT OF IT

This is a great object lesson you can use to illustrate—and the kids can use as a reminder—that we are to be separate from the world.

Give each child a key ring and two pieces of black ribbon and one piece of red ribbon. (Depending on the time you have and the age of the kids the ribbon can already be tied onto the key rings.) Instruct the kids to put black beads on the black ribbon and clear beads on the red ribbon. Ask the kid what they think black represents (sin) and what the red represents (the blood of Jesus). Then explain how the red ribbon and clear beads represents them. Even though the world is covered in sin they can be separate and holy for God in the midst of the sinful world.

Pray for God to forgive you for any of your sins, and forgive those who have done wrong to you.

COUNTRY PRAYER

The idea for this activity is to pray and discuss how your country can become more pleasing to God. Below are some steps you can use but feel free to do them in any order you would like, or change and add to it.

- Give the kids paper and markers. Instruct them to make a new country. Write the laws you would like to have in your country and make a flag for the country.

- Gather the kids back together and discuss what their countries are like. Allow for sharing.

- Talk about the laws and freedoms in your country vs. other countries.

- Ask what a country created by God would look like. What kind of laws would there be?

- Have a listening time and ask God how we can pray for our country (that we live in) to become more like He would want.

OIL SPILL PRAYER

The oil spill off the Gulf Coast of the United States had an affect on many people. It affected jobs, the price of oil, wildlife, the ocean, and even land.

One kids prayer group prayed about the oil spill and its effects. Their leader put together a PowerPoint presentation with pictures and some brief points about what has happened with the oil spill. To show the affects that oil had, she used a bowl that had water in it and poured oil on the top. Then she placed a rubber duck in the water to show how the oil attaches to everything around it. The group then shared ideas of what they could pray and spent time in doing so.

Since children love animals, include animals in your examples. Kids will love to pray for them.

A BUCKET OF PRAYER

If you have had a kids prayer group for a while it can become hard to reinforce prayer basics that they've already learned, without the kids becoming bored. This is where a bucket of prayer can be helpful.

On slips of paper write down different prayer activities your group has done and place them in a bucket (any container will work).

For example a local prayer group that did this had things such as: pick a worship song; globe prayers, bean bag prayers, bow and arrow, and listening time.

Have a child pick a slip of paper and the whole group will participate in whatever is printed on the paper. This will give some variety and make the reviewing the basics fun again, since the ideas came from them.

MK (MISSIONARY KIDS) PRAYER PALLS

Would you like to help the kids in your Sunday school class, prayer group or even at home become more active in praying for the Kingdom? One way to do this is to adopt a MK (Missionary Kid).

MK's are just like the kids we come in contact with on a day-to-day basis. They love to play, talk with friends, eat pizza, and have a desire to be used in ministry. However MK's are in need of some extra spiritual support and friendship. Many MK's consider the country where their family is serving as home. So when they come back to their home nation on deputation, they may feel homesick and lonely. Some kids go to the missionary field when they are older and the opposite happens. They are homesick and lonesome for their friends back in their home nation. Sometimes MK's just are not sure where they fit in.

By becoming a MK Prayer Pal you and the children you work with have a chance to make a huge impact on the world. When kids are on the mission field with their parents they also take on responsibilities and ministry in the church. They become musicians, Sunday school teachers and some even preach. They need extra prayer covering because the enemy thinks he can take them out quicker because they are young. Sometimes an MK does drift away from God even when they are surrounded by miracles. Your kids can be the encouragement that makes a difference in a MK's day, possibly even in their life.

It is very simple to get involved. Visit the website **upwithmks.com**. You will find a link to view a recent list of MKs. Pick an MK or two and get in contact them using the address information supplied. If you can't find their address information, send a contact message through the website and someone will assist you.

Write to the MK and ask them to send you stories about what is happening in their country. Tell them what you and your kids are doing as well.

By becoming a prayer pal with an MK you are giving them instant friendship. Be sure to consistently pray for them and their family. Encourage them and let them know that they are important to the Kingdom of God, and to you!

BUILDING PRAYERS

It is important to build an altar in your life and it is also important for children to understand this concept. When teaching this to various children we asked the kids if they knew any stories from the Bible that talked about altars. We asked the kids what an altar was. Then we shared the story in Joshua chapter four about the altar that was built after crossing into the promise land. We also shared what an altar was to us (the teachers).

While we were talking we allowed the kids to build altars using Magnetix (you can use anything that will stack to build, such as blocks, or Legos). By the time we had read the Scripture reference and all shared in the question and answer time the kids had each built an altar. Each one looked slightly different.

This activity helped illustrate that while there is an altar at church we each need an altar in our life and that each one will look different

ADORATION ALPHABET

The Adoration Alphabet is a fun and easy way to teach kids about worship. This ideas has been adapted from the book "When Children Pray" by Cheri Fuller. This is an activity that could be used monthly during your focus on worship.

Write a letter of the alphabet on a piece of poster board that has been cut into quarters. You can also use index cards for smaller versions. On the opposite side have kids write down as many words that they can think of that can be used as praise to/about God and that start with that letter. Then have each kids say as many of the words as they can in one breath.

For another exercise you could go in a circle starting with the letter "A" and say a word of praise to God. Then the next person repeats that word and adds one with the letter "B". Keep going until someone forgets or can't come up with a word. This is a project that you can spread out over a year. Once you have the whole alphabet, use the letters to spell out worship words.

Here are some of the answers some kids came up with. T- trustworthy, truthful, terrific, triumphant Z - zealous U - unique, unlimited, ultimate, understanding, undeniable X - x-cellent, x-tra special, x-treme, x-alted, x-tra large, x-ray vision

T.H.U.M.B.- O. PRAYING (M&M PRAYERS)

Praying THUMBO prayers will help the people living in the 10x40 Window! (Visit win1040.com for more information)

The "10/40 Window." This is an area of the world that has the most people living in it, but the fewest Christians and/or missionaries. It is located 10 degrees north of the equator and runs up to 40 degrees north of the equator. It spans from Korea through northern Africa.

This idea comes mostly from material produced by the "Caleb Project" (calebproject.org) with the addition of the letter "O." THUMB-O prayers help children pray for particular people groups by religion. These false religions are spiritual strongholds and are currently blocking efforts of Christians to evangelize this area of the world. THUMB-O prayers cover the major religions found in the 10/40 Window. The added "O" is for orphans, which we have found to be a very tender spot for children from any country.

Here is a suggestion on how to use the M&M colors to help you pray:

BROWN = TRIBAL—people filled with fear, who worship animals, and objects.

GREEN = MUSLIMS—they believe Jesus is only a prophet or good man, and that Allah is God.

RED = HINDU—worships millions of gods.

ORANGE = BUDDHISTS—they try to do good works on their own but it doesn't get them to heaven.

YELLOW = UNRELIGIOUS—they do not believe in any god.

BLUE = ORPHANS—children all over the world without parents who need someone to care and provide a Christian home for them.

PRAYING IN THE PARK

Spring, summer, or fall is a great time of year to take a group of children on a prayer walk in the park. Lead them in prayer for their city, neighborhoods, schools, friends, church, pastor, children of the world, etc.

If there are people in the park, two or three of the children (with adult supervision) could approach them explaining they have gathered together for prayer and inquire if they have a special request.

Encourage the children to pray for/with people immediately or, if they are a little shy, take the requests back to the group to be prayed over.

PRAYER REMINDERS

Often in spite of good intentions to pray more each day, the time slips by and we haven't prayed. Here are some "crutches" that can be used to remind us to pray at different times.

1. In the morning, as school bus' come or pass by you house, it can remind you to pray for the safety of students, teachers and other school employees.

2. When you read the newspaper, check the hospital list; it can remind you to pray for those who are ill and those who care for the ill. Look at the obituaries and pray for the hurting family members of the deceased.

3. When you hear a siren or see an emergency vehicle, pray for those who in pain or danger. Pray for wisdom for their doctors and caregivers.

4. At the grocery store, pray for the people you see. As you put food in your cart, pray for those less fortunate and for those who are hungry.

This list could go on and on. Each day, look for your own reminders and opportunities for prayer.

START A PRAYER TRIPLET

Based on Matthew 18:19-20, a prayer triplet is a simple convenient way to win people to Christ.

First, choose two Christian friends or relatives to make your triplet. Each of you choose the names of three people who need salvation, and choose a country or people group where Jesus' name is not known. Agree on a time to meet once a week to pray together - just 15 minutes at home, at work, at school, before or after a meeting is all it takes.

Pray together for the nine people (by name) for salvation and their personal needs. Also pray for the country and people group chosen.

Involve yourself with the three people you have chosen to pray for as much as possible. Have the triplet members pray for each other as well.

As your friends become Christians, continue to pray for them as well as for new unsaved friends.

CHRISTMAS PRAYER BOX

Have your children decorate a shoebox and place it on the dining room table. Place Christmas cards or photos that you receive during the holiday season in this box. At meal times, or during your devotions, have a child pull a card out of the box and pray for the family who sent it. Talk about any special needs that person or family may have at that time.

For a group of children, you can have them bring in cards from home, or leave a box in the church foyer for people to drop prayer requests into that the children can pray for.

PRAY OVER THE CHURCH ANNOUNCEMENTS

For a quick or different way to pray, take the church announcements and pray over them. State the announcement then have the children prayer together over the event.

Examples:

"Vacation Bible School will begin in June." Pray for God's blessing on the activity. Pray that the hearts of the children will be ripe to hear about God. Pray for guidance, direction and anointing on the workers.

"Outreach will be Saturday morning at 10:00AM." Pray that God will help each person to see the need for outreach and that they will be burdened for lost souls. Pray that all will be safe as they knock on doors. Pray that hearts will be open to hear the gospel and that hungry souls will want to come to know Jesus Christ.

PRAYER CROWD-BREAKER

Divide your group into teams. Give each team a piece of paper and a pen. In five minutes have each team write down as many prayer requests that they can think of. (ex. Lost family members, healings, church growth, pastor, world needs, school issues, community concerns, missionaries, etc.)

At the end of five minutes count the requests and award a prize to the winning team. Then copy the prayer list and distribute them to the kids prayer group members, and have them pray over the list for the week.

Check back the following week to see which prayers were answered, and give God a celebration of thanks for it!

PRAYER FOR WORLD NEEDS

Form groups of no more than four and give each group a newspaper section filled with world news. Say: "Your group has 5 minutes to search your newspaper for one situation you want us to pray for, such as gang violence, drugs, famine, floods, or earthquakes."

After 5 minutes, gather the groups and have them discuss their selection. Pray for each world need. At completion of prayer time read John 16:33.

Create a "World Prayer Needs" bulletin board. Throughout the week have kids cut out magazine or newspaper articles containing world needs that they want the group to pray for. Have them tack the articles to the bulletin board as visual prayer reminders.

WASHED AWAY

Each kid is given a washable marker. On the palm of their hands have them write one thing they want washed away from their lives. (Example: gossip, lying, cheating, disobedience, or secular music.)

Bring out a basin of water, soap and a towel. Discuss the importance of repenting during our prayer time and how sin separates us from God. Discuss how we can wash our hands of dirt and be clean, but we will not remain clean if we keep going back to the mud pit and play in it—we have to stay away from it.

Have each person repent of the sin or issue, and pray for God to give them help and strength to change and turn away from the habit or problem. After or during prayer, have them wash their hands or even those of a neighbor, symbolizing how God washes away our sin when we repent.

MUSICAL PRAYERS

Spread around pieces of paper on the floor with things written on them to pray or give thanks for (e.g. shout a name for God three times, thank God for your best mate, sing one chorus of a song, be silent for 30 seconds). Then play bouncing, loud music as everyone bounces around musically, from square to square on the floor until the music stops and you have to follow the instructions.

It's important for the young people to hear each other pray and praise God. This will build faith, and bring encouragement for them to participate also when it is their turn

Other suggestions for the pieces of paper:

- Shout out one thing you are grateful for.

- Stop, ask God what He wants to share with the child or the group.

- Simply tell God about your day.

- Ask God for something you want or need.

- Ask God for something for one of your friends.

- Thank God for another person in your life.

- Ask God to help someone in the hospital.

- Shout out the name of someone you hope to become a Christian, and pray for them.

- Tell God something you want forgiveness for.

- Tell God someone you want to forgive.

Add some of your own prayer requests or needs of others.

PAPER TOWEL PRAYERS

The prayer leader begins by unrolling a roll of paper towels on the floor. Using a black marker, have each person write a person's name or prayer concern on each sheet. Re-roll. Each day, or each kids prayer meeting, tear off one sheet and have the children lift up prayers for that particular concern or person.

As the sheets are prayed over, tear them off and pin them to a wall or area where others can see the prayers that are being made. This will encourage them to pray as well.

You can also save the paper towel cardboard roll and see how many you can collect through an entire year.

NAIL-A-PRAYER

Build a wooden cross (the size will depend on size of your group.) Give each child one or more post-it notes or pieces of paper to write a prayer request on. With the help of an adult, have each child nail that concern on the cross. You can also use tacks and pin the papers to a cross posted on a bulletin board or wall if you don't wish to use a wooden cross.

As an alternative, have the child write a problem that they are struggling with on the paper, such as disobedience, or something that they are afraid of or have been hurt over. Students at a Christian Bible college did this idea using a wooden cross and cardboard signs that they wrote their testimonies and struggles on. As they played the song "Orphans of God" by Avalon, each student came during their turn and nailed their sign to the cross. God touched them in profound ways as they gave their concerns and worship to Him for what He done in their lives, and what He was doing at that moment. God's blood still covers our sin!

HAND PRAYERS

Trace the child's hand on a piece of paper.

On the thumb write "praise and worship," (Psalm 147:1).

On the pointer finger, write "confess our sins,"(1 John 1:8-9).

On the tallest finger write "thanking God," (Philippians 4:6; Psalm 136:1).

Write "needs of others" on the ring finger, (1 Timothy 2:1-4).

Finally, the pinky is the least of our fingers yet the most essential for having a strong grip. Write "our needs" on the pinky finger, (1 John 3:22).

Pray for each type of request, using the fingers, one at a time.

OUTREACH

Get a list of visitors that attended your church the past week and pray for them and their families.

You can have the children pray for them:

- to understand God's truth of salvation if they don't already.

- for God to draw them back to church again if they've left.

- for them to find God's purpose in their life.

- for their health and needs.

- for peace in their family.

- that God would provide their needs, etc.

Send them a card letting them know the kids prayer group and church is praying for them, and that someone cares about their life.

A TWIST ON PRAYER

One of the old games that children still love to play is Twister. During the game, each player spins a spinner and moves their hand or foot to whatever color the spinner lands on. It's a crazy game of twisting your body to get to the right spot.

You can modify this game by taping prayer requests to the different colored circles. These can be focused requests such as for specific countries, people groups, or other Kingdom prayers.

You can write personal or family requests, but just be sure to include requests for needs of God's Kingdom as well.

OPEN PRAYER JOURNAL

Purchase a spiral notebook and put the date of each Sunday in the top corner. Have the book open to the appropriate page each Sunday and displayed in a prominent place. Encourage the children to write down any prayer requests or praise report as they arrive each Sunday. They can also look at previous pages to see what prayers were answered. The journal can be referred to during class prayer time, or the requests can be reviewed at the end of class and given to the children to pray for during the week.

You can also have one of these journals for the adults to put their prayer requests into as they enter church foyer. At the end of service, collect the journal and have the children pray over the requests that the adults mentioned. Be sure to write down whatever God shares with the children regarding a request they prayed about. God speaks to children just as He does adults.

PRAYER MEDICS

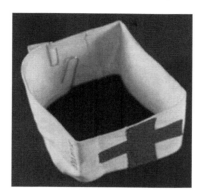

Military branches of service have personnel who are called "Medics." They have the job of attending to injured soldiers on the battlefield. Often Medics are designated by wearing a white band with a red cross or crescent on their arm and/or helmet.

Explain to the children that each of us are called to be medics at times in God's Kingdom—in His war. We become medics by praying for the needs of others, and reaching out to those around us with love and comfort.

Make white armbands out of fabric with red crosses on them for each child. Have them tie the armbands on and then pray over needs that are mentioned. Include Kingdom needs since we are medics in God's army.

Be sure to explain the importance of their job as a medic. If a medic does not take the time or effort to help (pray) then lives can be lost.

EMPTY CHAIR PRAYERS

We all know people who do not come to church or live a Christian life. Have the child write the name of such a person, or bring in a photo of them. They may bring more than one if desired.

Set an empty chair in the middle of the group. If the group is already sitting in chairs then just have an extra one that can be left empty. Have the child put the paper with the person's name or photo that they brought, on the seat of the chair. Have the child or group of children pray for God to help that person realize their need of Him and bring the person salvation.

In addition, you can pray for those who feel lonely, abandoned, or those who feel like no one cares for them. Pray for God to let them feel His love and comfort. Pray that God to each child them to be friendly and loving to those around them, including other children who may feel friendless.

LEAVE IT BEHIND

Kids are often playing video games within twenty minutes of being home from school or church. They can end up playing for hours at a time. Kids will always have playtime, but they must know that playing is not more important than prayer.

Have the children bring in their hand-held games one night during your kids prayer session. Tell them the previous week that they will get to have game time during the next week's session and to bring their games with them. (Be sure to tell them that they should only be playing video games that are approved by their parents and that are appropriate for them to be playing.) Most kids will be very excited about having this opportunity.

On game day, give them a designated amount of time to play and interact with each other. At the end of the game time, collect their games and keep them for a week. Let the parents know ahead of time you are doing this. Explain to them that this week they are to give the time that they normally play games to prayer, reading their bible and listening as God speaks to them. The next week, talk about how much time they found they had wasted just playing games.

HALLOWEEN PRAYER CANDY

If your children's families participate in handing out Halloween candy then you can encourage them to hand out "Prayer Candy" instead. Have children pray over the bowls of candy that are handed out and write prayers or scriptures on pieces of paper to put in another bowl. As children come to the door to receive their candy, give them the candy that's been prayed over along with a prayer/scripture strip or even a card to invite them to church or to your kids prayer meeting.

If your church does an activity at church instead, you can still pray over the candy and give out the prayer/scripture strips as well.

WATCH-N-PRAY

It's been said that "a picture is worth a thousand words." Since many people are more visually minded and have taken hundreds of photos to relive memories, why not incorporate that into your kid's prayer time?

As your kids pray for people that you know, bring in a video camera and videotape them praying. Send a copy of that video to the person you prayed for so they can see and hear how much there are cared for.

If you do not have a video camera, or if the children are too shy to pray on camera, then simply take a photo of them praying for that person during that time and send it instead.

Often people will keep those photos as memories and it will bring them strength and encouragement at later times.

COMMUNITY PRAYER MAPS

Another way to get children praying for the needs of others is to have them pray for their community.

Bring in paper for them to draw a map of their community, showing where their house is, their friend's house, the school, the playground, etc. Let them color the maps if there is time and use this as prayer tool. Pray for each area, business, school, or home.

For some children this may appear to be a little difficult, so you can have them draw a picture of their house with different rooms where their family members live instead. Pray for each family member, or those who come to visit them at their home.

BREAKING CHAINS

Purchase a piece of chain and a padlock from any do-it-yourself store, such as Home Depot. Let the children feel the weight of the chain and the lock. Discuss how hard the chain and lock is, and how cold, and heavy it would be to carry around all day long. Discuss how the chains can rub the skin of ankles and wrist raw until the person is bleeding or infected. Discuss how chains make it difficult to move around and be free.

As they feel the weight, coldness and hardness of it, have them to pray for those who live in slavery today, such as the thousands of women and children who are still enslaved in North Sudan. Discuss how slavery separates families and can cause death for those in bondage. Pray for those who are enslaving others, that they would set them free.

Talk about how addictions to drugs, alcohol and other things enslave people and keep them from being free in their spirit. Pray for freedom, and for God to break the addictions and help the person repent and turn away from their sinful lifestyle.

LIGHT YOUR WORLD

There is a large area of the world known as the 10/40 Window where there are the least number of Christians, and where the gospel is least preached, if at all.

Talk to your children about the privilege they have in knowing about God and being able to read the Bible and pray openly when so many others in the 10/40 Window cannot.

Turn off the lights, and have them pray for these areas and these people.

Pray for ministers to go and share the gospel, for the Bible to be allowed in the areas, and for God to fill them with His Spirit.

As each child prays their turn, have them crack a light stick or turn on a flashlight to show how God's light and truth bring understanding through prayer and revelation.

STICKS AND STONES

The world is full of people who have been hurt by words and actions of other people. Some of them are around you. The words we say and the actions we do can either build us up or tear us down. They can hurt our spirit and self-image.

Take small, smooth stones and have each child write something that has hurt them or something that they have done to hurt someone else. Write a word describing that on the stone with a permanent marker.

You may also write it on a small strip of cloth and tie around some sticks.

Have the children hold the sticks/stones and pray that God would forgive them for anything they've said that has hurt someone else, as well as ask God to heal their heart from things others have told them. Have them ask God to help them see themselves through His eyes and to understand how He feels about them.

When you are done praying, review with the children that sticks and stones (like the ones they are holding) hurt people and we must be careful to treat others as God treats us—with love and good words.

PRAYER SKETCHES

Often it's easier for a child to draw what they are feeling or wanting to express rather than describing it in words, especially if they are younger or if they are shy.

Occasionally have your children pray and use drawing in the process. They can either pray and listen to what they feel God is sharing with them and draw it, or they start drawing out something they are feeling. When they are done drawing, an adult can help them "interpret" what they can pray for depending on what was drawn.

For example, a child may pray and feel like God was showing them a color, a person, a place or an event. They begin to draw out what God was sharing with them or what they were feeling. Sometimes playing soft music in the background while the children are drawing helps them to focus.

One drawing was of a person with scratches and marks all around them. This was a reflection of the troubles and chaos they were feeling. Another drew a kitty cat, which was sick and had made the child worried.

YOUR IDEAS

List some of your own ideas.

_____

_____

_____

_____

_____

_____

_____

_____

_____

_____

_____

_____

_____

_____

_____

_____

_____

_____

_____

_____

_____

_____

_____

_____

_____

_____

_____

_____

YOUR IDEAS

List some of your own ideas.

_____

_____

_____

_____

_____

_____

_____

_____

_____

_____

_____

_____

_____

_____

_____

_____

_____

_____

_____

_____

_____

_____

_____

_____

_____

YOUR IDEAS

List some of your own ideas.

_____

_____

_____

_____

_____

_____

_____

_____

_____

_____

_____

_____

_____

_____

_____

_____

_____

_____

_____

_____

_____

_____

_____

_____

YOUR IDEAS

List some of your own ideas.

_____

_____
_____
_____
_____
_____
_____
_____
_____
_____
_____
_____
_____
_____
_____
_____
_____
_____
_____
_____
_____
_____
_____
_____
_____
_____

_____

Colleen Clabaugh is the Kids and Youth Prayer Coordinator for the World Network of Prayer, an international prayer ministry.

She is a mother of two wonderful boys, a speaker, and a writer of many books and resources on prayer, and currently runs the Kids Prayer ministry at her local church.

Made in the USA
San Bernardino, CA
20 November 2013